53 CROSS STREET

Biography of a House

by

Mary Cosh and Martin King

Photographs by Pauline Lord

Islington Archaeology and History Society

2007

Published 2007 by **Islington History and Archaeology Society**
8 Wynyatt Street, London EC1V 8UH

© the respective authors
© colour photographs: Pauline Lord
© interior of house design and implementation by Martin King except where otherwise stated

ISBN 978-0-958490-0-9

The narrative of 53 Cross Street was written by Mary Cosh, based on Martin King's written
record. The paper on the hall stencil wall painting was written by Martin King in 1996 for
an MA in the History of Design at the Victoria and Albert Museum and the Royal College
of Art, with later revisions. The photographs, except where otherwise noted, were all taken
by Pauline Lord in 2003.

We are grateful to English Heritage for permission to reproduce the frontispiece and
endpapers, to the British Museum Prints and Drawings Collection for the painting by
George Scharf (page 69) with special thanks to Amelia Jackson for her care in tracing the
original; and Islington Local History Library for the 1835 engraving (pages 70–1).

We are also particularly grateful to Tracy Wellman for her skilled presentation and
production of the whole.

Front cover
Shows Martin King's re-creation of the original stencil wall painting
against photograph of ground floor front room © Pauline Lord

Contents

Illustrations

6   53 Cross Street, Exterior North Elevation, view from across the street

A brief history of the house

Mary Cosh

The four-storey terrace now numbered 53–59 Cross Street was built by March 1785, no.53, lowest of the four, then being numbered 25. Its top floor was added only after the Napoleonic Wars, and it was shown in a watercolour of 1816 by George Scharf in his first London painting. The house appears again in 1835 in a view from the top of Canonbury Tower. It became no.53 in a renumbering in 1862, when Mr James Cook was the occupier.

In 1871 John Tiley, a brass engraver, his wife Elizabeth and two (eventually eleven) children moved there from Clerkenwell, and he set up his engraving workshop in the house and in an outhouse at the back (as disclosed in the 1990s by their great-great-granddaughter Sue Peacock), shown in the 1871 Ordnance map.

Later in the 19th century, as shown on OS 1894, half the garden was taken over for the site of St Mary's parish church hall. A brassworks outhouse was built in the backyard late in the century, together with an outside lavatory. Gas lighting was introduced – traces of the pipes survive on bedroom walls – and in the downstairs living-room a cast-iron fireplace was installed. Many of the finds later made by Martin King date from the 1850s–60s (see under *The Discoveries*).

The saddest decades in the house's history began in the 1950s, when it was in increasingly forlorn condition. The floors were covered with layers of worn lino, disfigured by stiletto marks. Signs of children in the 60s were shown by small lost possessions – a tiny plastic coin in old currency, a tinier plastic mouse, both fallen through the floorboards of Martin's bedroom, and a broken stiletto heel; while a number of film spools in the basement suggested that it might have been used as a darkroom. All of it lost or abandoned rubbish; everywhere signs of neglect.

In 1978 Islington Council compulsorily purchased, but were unable to afford restoration, and for the next half-dozen years the four houses remained empty, occasionally squatted. By 1980 the row was literally decaying. At no.53 the roof leaked, on both second and top floors some of the ceilings fell in, besides in the basement and lavatory.

"Cowboy developers" converted the whole row nos 53–59 into bed-sits, by the simple expedient of covering over old features, nailing up shutters and boarding over the cellar walls with wood-chip. The 1950s occupants were Maltese sailors, and by 1983 "punk anarchists", during all which time the terrace had continued to deteriorate.

The great change came in 1983, when the Council handed over nos 53 and 59 to the Black Sheep Housing Co-op (a group of "Anarchist punk squatters", as Martin King puts it) – exuberantly described by the *Evening Standard* as "loony left" in an attack on the Council. Much to the indignation of the *Standard* who castigated the Council for their decision, these obtained six-month leases on the two houses and made basic repairs. Roofs and ceilings were given much-needed repairs, the walls were repointed, and the interior painted in colourful varieties (a couple of the jobs still remain). In the early 90s the house was painted white.

In 1990 a tenant who moved in was Martin King, a young cultural studies lecturer at the Central St Martin's College of Art and Design. It was 19th October, his 30th birthday. While he found living at no.53 more or less on the level of camping, he soon became fascinated by the history – in all senses – of the house.

That Christmas, reading John Richardson's *Islington Past*[*] he found it contained pictures of the house, dated 1816 and 1835. He longed to find out more, though there was a suspicion that all would soon be moved out. But it filled his mind with thoughts of Islington's rural past, and he wondered if William Blake, or later Charles Dickens, had ever passed them by.

Meanwhile the Council's proposal was to sell the houses to a housing association for a mere £11,111, which caused a local outcry at the price – when the (admittedly considerably larger and grander) no.61 was on the market for more than £1 ¹/₂ million.

For the other houses of the little terrace the object was to do them up, and to redevelop the fish-and-chip shop at the corner of Dagmar Passage (1989). One Councillor, however, Richard Heseltine, urged overall restoration of the whole four houses nos 53–59, each also considered worth £1 ¹/₂ million, as a kind of "rich man's row".

In November 1993 the Heritage of London Trust showed interest in buying the row, but though Islington Council was favourable, provided the existing shortlife tenants could stay on, negotiations dragged on for years. Meanwhile in September Martin had tried, unsuccessfully, to trace the original house deeds at the Greater London Record Office, and for the next two years was engaged in a serious 'excavation' of the house, vertically and horizontally.

The discoveries

On return from a summer's long stay in a historic farmhouse in Wales, Martin started to explore the fabric of his own house. Did the living-room contain a fireplace? Indeed it did. The wall hid not only a cast-iron late Victorian fireplace but masked six binbags of soot, three skeletal pigeons and some coal surviving from its last fire in the 1950s.

Removing the 1950s wood-chip coverings, releasing nailed-up shutters and stripping walls

---

[*]Historical Publications, 1980.

back to their original surfaces, brought remarkable, indeed unique discoveries.

For example, stripping the wood-chip bedroom walls exposed 18th-century plaster, revealing faint traces of stencilled fresco, and the hardwood covering revealed the 18th-century panelled door. One doorway proved to lead to two rooms whose walls had been pierced by tree-roots from the garden. The temporary cellar walls, put up in the 1950s to contrive a squalid bathroom, proved to be a shoddy cover for a large, intact, original scullery containing a copper boiler.

Under the bedroom floorboards early in 1994 Martin found a postcard dated 13 March 1897 addressed to "J. Tiley Esquire". Also under the floorboards were brass engineering offcuts, evidence of a brass engraver's occupation of the house. Martin identified this family from the Cross Street records in the Public Record Office, Chancery Lane: "brass engraver and letter maker".

Only a few days later, looking out of the window he saw a man photographing the house, and on going out to talk to him and his wife, discovered that the wife's great-great-grandfather had lived there. To their astonishment he asked, "Oh, you mean John Tiley?" – a most uncanny surprise coincidence for both parties. (Sue Peacock, the wife, corrected his pronunciation of the name.) A week later she called again, with her husband and sister, and told Martin that Tiley brasswork survived in some Islington churches, even in St Paul's Cathedral – though they had never seen any of it.

He showed his visitors the brass offcuts, and collages he had made with them. One engraving was "a small gothic cross with IHC inscribed in the centre, perhaps discarded because the lettering ought to have read "IHS", for "in hoc signo" (or for "IHSUS", as on the Cross). This piece, ironically, was "the sole completed engraving that can be definitely attributed to the Tiley workshop".

The family gave him a photograph of their forebears in the backyard in 1913, and he now saw the faces of the man who had lived there a hundred years before and of his daughters, two of whom had been born there. They had by 1913 lived there for 52 years, and the daughters their whole lives; but next year they moved away, leaving their traces under floorboards and in a family album . . . to be discovered now by "a homespun historian".

In March 1994, again under floorboards, Mark found walnut shells left by 18th-century workmen, and learned from a friend that walnuts and watercress would have been a workman's staple diet. Could these have been remains of George Shaw's – the possible builder's – lunches, four years before the French Revolution?

Next, below his living-room floorboards he found a 1950s lightbulb box, pierced by a mousehole, probably once containing rat-poison: was this in the 1950s a rodent-infested old house? Also a late-19th-century card advertising Johnston's Patent Cornflour with, on its other side, an illustration from *Martin Chuzzlewit*. "Dickens's London mirrored in its own advertising," he thought. "I wonder if Dickens ever looked at this house as he walked past. He was quite observant."

That summer he replaced two of the 1950s living-room doors with 18th-century panelled doors found in the backyard. "As hard as stone, stripped by the weather," the house timber was deal, from some Scandinavian forest over 200 years ago. After that he started stripping the living-room's wood-chip paper, to remarkable effect. Then in the autumn, his varied house finds from over two centuries, all of which, however trivial-seeming, he had scrupulously kept, were exhibited in Islington's small new museum. They were subsequently intended as a permanent deposit.

Then there was the garden. Here Martin dug up old door-handles, brass engravings, and remains of the original house doors. The former garden also contained remains of a wrecked war-time air-raid shelter and an outhouse, damaged where a bomb fell on the neighbouring St Mary's parish church. Another dig brought up brass offcuts from John Tiley's occupancy, clay pipes, broken marble pieces from the 18th-century fireplaces, the latter presumably destroyed in the 1950s 'modernisation'. There were also a 2nd-World-War gas-mask, and a 1940s woman's shoe behind the air-raid shelter.

Nothing was too trivial, too old or too new to escape Martin's interest. He scrupulously gathered every fragment, either to be re-used in partial restoration of the original house, or presented to the local museum.

Meanwhile he held two "Installations" in the basement to display his findings, leading to an interested review of the house in *Time Out*. An artist, Crow, found a pendulum and a key wrapped in a triangular piece of black nylon cloth, behind the chipboard wall covering.

In July 1993, digging with a house-mate, Mark McAuley, in the backyard, they turned up (he tells us) "an early 19th-century ink bottle, bits of brass, a 19th-century iron, pottery fragments, numerous oyster shells underneath the fireplace in the workshop . . . fragments of clay pipes and a 1923 farthing".

Below a layer of dark earth, about a foot underground, was the 19th-century layer. Two feet down they found a piece of a clay pipe shaped as "a mid-19th-century Romantic female figure". Three feet down, a scrap of lead roofing. He fancied he might even uncover the core of Isledon, Islington's Saxon ancestor, which was only a short space behind the house. Or might the whole dig collapse and bury him? It seemed safer to concentrate on the house.

So in August 1993 he opened the nailed-up living-room shutters, closed for a hundred years and still with their 19th-century soot-covered brown paint. Shining a torch through the wall cavity, with a mirror, he saw two sooty pieces of material scattered with long wood shavings, and by means of a nail on the end of a piece of wood he managed to hook them out. They proved to be some sort of stockings. Inside one was (he says) "a piece of unprimed wood moulding (possibly used for the original windows as there are no similar mouldings in the rest of the house), and, written in pencil in very neat copperplate handwriting, 'George Shaw went to Aameica March 1785'." Just when the house was first built. He would be the carpenter, or possibly builder, of the house, probably using his profit from the new building to pay for the voyage. Martin felt amazement at this unforeseen, uncanny communication between two strangers "in the same room, separated by 208 years" where Shaw had left his "time-capsule" (page 14).

"The leggings were heavily darned, had blood stains and had been worn by somebody with very thin legs." The long wood-shavings showed good craftsmanship, and their dry, sound preservation demonstrated the house builders' skill.

The wall-coverings

In the late 1990s, along with Mark McAuley, Martin uncovered much of the original fabric of the house, that had been covered in the 1950s and 60s in hardboard and wood-chip paper. As he went along, he kept fragments of the layers of wallpaper stretching back to the early 19th century (see pages 26–31), and in 1996 he found in the hall, underneath seven layers of wallpaper, the original stencil wall painting of 1785.

As can be seen from the illustration, it is in a remarkable state of preservation. Martin wrote an essay on the composition of the stencil, as part of his MA in Design History at the Royal College of Art. It is reproduced here on pages 51–69.

In the year 2000, English Heritage undertook a detailed photographic record of the house. From Martin's point of view the most valuable photographs were of a second 1785 wall stencil design, fragments of which were found on the bare plaster walls of the two ground-floor and two first-floor rooms (see page 20). With the aid of tracing paper and coloured pencils, he was actually able to re-create the original designs.

In the basement, he also uncovered original paint-work of 1785: pale blue on the plastered walls, a creamy stone colour on the woodwork. Thus, by the time he left Cross Street, Martin had a remarkably complete record of the decor of the house from its building date onwards, including many of the succeeding layers of wall-decoration.

The outcome

Such discoveries, through stripping a modest late-18th-century terrace house back to its original surfaces, were so unusual – almost unique – that it was too good to be kept quiet.

He started by inviting groups of his students to visit, and as the story spread, took 'conducted tours'. He also enlisted the help of his MP, Chris Smith, then Culture Secretary, who proved very supportive. The remarkable story was written up in the *Evening Standard*, the *Observer Magazine*, and the then two local papers, *Islington Gazette* and *Highbury and Islington Express*, and the house was described on television and radio. Yet Martin knew that his occupancy was always on sufferance.

In May 2001, by means of photocopies, Martin exhibited the reconstructed stencil, in the ground-floor front room (pages 13, 20) as an art installation for the "Out of the Void" exhibition by artists in short-life housing.

The looming threat had become imminent. By 1999 the Council was hoping to sell to Heritage of London Trust, and by the summer of 2001 the end seemed nigh. Once the Council's short-life housing had ended that January, Black Sheep Housing Co-op staged a grand farewell-cum-publicity party, with videos and talks, and every such co-op was issued with a two-year lease, prior to sale of their houses on the open market. This led to a new flurry of publicity, now including also the *Sunday Express*, the *Guardian Weekend* and *The Big Issue*.

By this time Martin was aware that the new Liberal Democrat Islington Council leadership were committed to selling nos 53–59 Cross Street on the open market, rendering the existing tenants homeless. He had already been campaigning for some years for 53–59 to remain in social housing, and for the existing short-life tenants to gain secure tenancies. He now embarked on a media campaign, using his historical project as a means of promoting awareness of the desperate situation of Islington's 500 short-life tenants threatened with homelessness.

Martin lived out his notice, still taking conducted tours. Living had continued under difficult conditions: contrived kitchen, DIY shower, open fireplaces. Overgrown shrubs had formed a thicket outside this Aladdin's cave with its unique treasures – not silver and gold but broken, forgotten possessions from the past, all hinting at their history.

Finally, after a series of farewell parties attended by journalists, TV personalities, neighbours who had known the house in earlier days, pop groups and friends, in March 2003 Martin moved out to temporary Council accommodation.

Even though Martin was briefly made homeless in 2003, thanks to the campaign he had initiated, he and his fellow short-life tenants and most of Islington's other short-life tenants now faced a more secure future.

By June 2003, Martin King was happily back in a flat a mere stone's-throw from the house which he had re-discovered and whose past he had evoked in such a loving re-creation, as a kind of ghost of itself. It was later sensitively, not over-, restored. Such a house we are hardly likely to find again.

Colour photographs of the interior

Pauline Lord

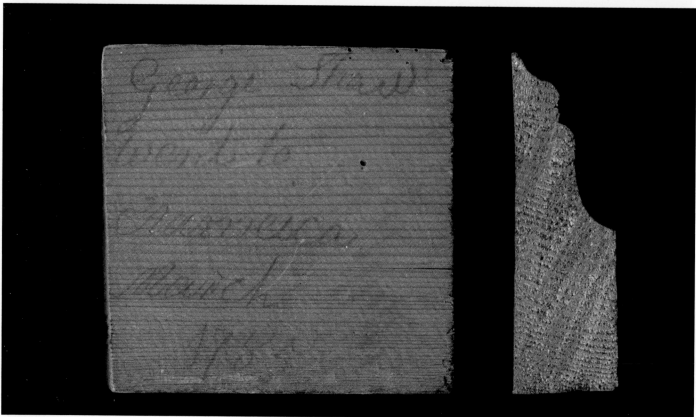

Stockings and block of wooden moulding inscribed "George Shaw went to Aameica March 1785"

Right Ground Floor Front Room showing original window shutters, walls stripped to original plaster, dado panelling; "Cabinet of Curiosities"; chandelier made by Martin King.

Ground Floor Front Room. Between the window shutters is Martin King's reconstruction of original 1785 wall stencil (2001), from the *Out of the Void Exhibition* by Islington Artists in Short-Life Housing. The green-painted woodwork reproduces the 1785 original. Fireplace removed in 1950s.

Doorway to Hall from ground floor front room. The 1870s Union Chapel noticeboard was found in a skip.

Ground Floor Front Room. Left-hand window showing shutter half closed and barred; modern hanging. 19th-century brown paint on shutters, green paint on window surround and panel by Martin King 2001; reproduction of original 1785 stencil wall painting.

Left View from ground floor front room to back. Wall panels painted by Martin King 1995.

Ground Floor Front Room: reconstruction of original 1785 stencil wall painting. This design was on the walls of both ground-floor rooms and the two first-floor rooms.

Right Ground Floor Front Room: "Cabinet of Curiosities". Items found by Martin King in house and back yard.

Cabinet of Curiosities, detail – *top:* 18th-century shelf; *bottom:* 19th-century shelf

Cabinet of Curiosities, detail – *top:* 20th-century shelf; *bottom:* 21st-century shelf

Ground Floor Back Rooom. Beside 19th-century fireplace is the brass-cutting machine found in back yard and probably used in this room. Walls stripped to original plaster; medallion: modern

24

Ground Floor Back Room – *top:* wall panelling, painted by Martin King 1995; *bottom:* looking towards window, showing original panelling

26   1950s wallpaper from former kitchen (ground floor back room)

Fragments of 1950s lino also from former kitchen

28   Original stencil wallpaper, top part-covered by 19th-century wallpaper, first-floor hall.

Layers of 19th-century wallpaper above stencil wall painting, first-floor hall 29

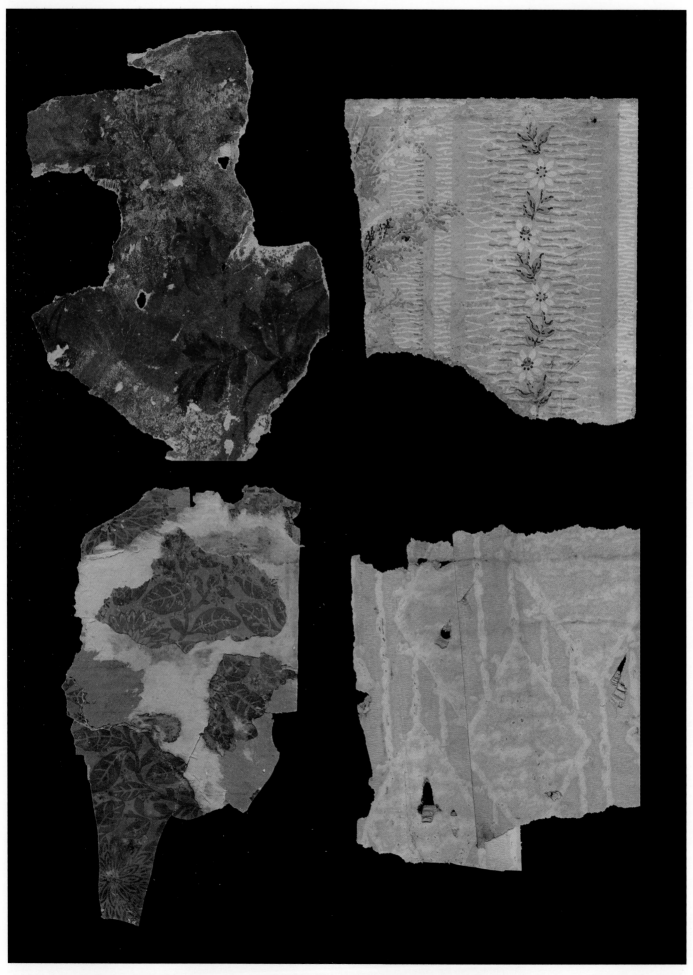

Wallpaper fragments – *top left:* 19th century, first floor hall; *top right:* 1940s front basement; *bottom left:* 19th century, dado panelling in ground floor hall; *bottom right:* ground floor front room

Wallpaper fragments – *top:* 19th century, ground floor front; *bottom left:* 1950s, basement front; *bottom right:* 1940s, first floor front

First Floor Back Room. Walls stripped; woodwork painted by Noam Zair 1997 (patch of green is original 1785 paint)

Left First Floor Back Room – *top:* looking towards St Mary's Parish Church Upper Street; original fireplace; panelling painted by Noam Zair 1999; *bottom:* opposite side of room

34   Second Floor Back Room: 18th-century door painted by Todd Hanson 1983

Second Floor Back Room: painted by Mark McAuley; fitted 19th-century sink

36   Second Floor Front Room: collage created by Matthew Appleton 1983

Wallpaper cuttings, 1940s/50s – *top left:* 3rd floor; *top right:* 1st floor hall; *bottom left:* 1st floor back; *bottom right:* 3rd floor hall

Third Floor Back. Panelling painted by Tim Taylor 1998

Left Third Floor Back Room: 1815 fireplace; wall stripped; panelling painted by
Tim Taylor 1998. Portrait of Chandy Lear, drag artist, by Mark McAuley 1993

Entrance Hall. View to rear staircase; walls stripped

Ground Floor to First Floor Staircase – two views: *top:* cut string design with decorative brackets; *bottom:* detail of newel

posts and panelling

Stairs at first floor landing – *top:* detail looking towards front of the house, Martin King at his desk; a replica of this room as it appeared in the late 18th century can be seen at the Geffrye Museum. Another view of handrail, newel posts and design of stairs: cut string with decorative brackets; *bottom:* Martin King with Les Swaine (BSHC member 1983–96); green panelling painted by Mark MacAuley 1997, on left

Second Floor Landing: detail of newel post

Half-landing 2nd/3rd-floor: detail showing old gas pipe

Half-landing 1st/2nd-floor: detail, opposite soffit visible in mirror

Basement Front Room: former kitchen; 19th-century fireplace, part-dismantled, replacing original range. Blue paint between windows facsimile of 1785 decoration by Martin King 1999

Basement Back Room: former scullery; original 18th-century copper (centre); 19th-century sink

Basement Back Room, former scullery: close-up of sink and copper

Right Basement Back Room, former scullery: Copper and 18th-century fireplace with remains of steam hood above

Martin King sheds light on the basement back room

A late 18th-century stencil wall painting at 53 Cross Street

Martin King, 1996

April 1996. I'm stripping wallpaper in my home (a late 18th-century terraced house), and find a stencilled wall painting. At first I wonder whether it's another layer of wallpaper, but as I carefully chisel away the layers on top of it I see colours which are much richer and more vibrant than any of the succeeding layers of brownish wallpaper. It is the blue that catches my eye at first (page 28). Slowly the isolated patches of colour give way to a recognisable image. I gradually reveal a representation of an arch covered in foliage with what appear to be Gothic cusps on the inside. The arch is supported by two unadorned pillars – a kind of rustic Tuscan Order without a base, resting instead on a ledge from which an exuberant bunch of flowers spills out. All these features, arch, foliage and flowers are picked out in a colour scheme of pale brown, dark green, black and white set against a sky-blue background.

As my chisel proceeds further, it reveals that the foliate arch is set in a wall of dark green brick. These are pierced on either side by a six-leaved Gothic detail filled in with blue. I soon discover that this basic pattern is repeated diagonally over the whole surface of the wall above the dado rail, in a very similar manner to wallpaper. It appears to be a stencil since breaks in the alignment are quite visible. The white is painted freestyle as the brush strokes are clearly visible and vary slightly from one part of the design to another.

The stencilled wall painting has been revealed side by side with fragments of six succeeding layers of wallpaper, ranging from Regency Marble brick effect wallpaper to faux wood, Victorian floral, Art Nouveau, and finally 1960s wood chip. Originally, it covered the whole of the plaster wall surface of the hall walls (the other surface being deal panelling). This covered approximately 33.48 square metres. One wall was completely replastered in the 1950s or 60s. In other parts of the hall, although the 18th-century plaster still remains, the stencil has been altered by successive redecoration. What remains is approximately 26.27 square metres, of which approximately 1.5 square metres has been uncovered. Although the stencil is chipped and has numerous holes (some of the most extensive damage was caused by electrical rewiring in the 1980s), it is in remarkably good condition. Nevertheless, two areas are at present being destroyed by damp.

One is approximately 2.5 square metres beside the front door; the other is approximately 1.5 square metres near the back door. At the time of writing (1996), there are only four other houses in London known to have stencil wall painting, none of which covers an area as large as the one at 53 Cross Street. The house is in the process of being bought by the Heritage of London Trust from Islington Council. This will give the house a more secure future and hopefully save the wall stencil from further erosion by damp.

So, despite the size and historical significance of the stencil, it is not a complete object, but a fragment. As a repeated pattern it is possible to imagine it as complete object, to imagine it where it no longer is. Indeed only a small area has been uncovered, yet I can imagine the hall as it was in the 18th century with its stone-coloured painted wood, the stencil, the staircase with the few missing banisters replaced, and the distant echo of long-silent voices. The light of the sun has cast the same shadows across the floorboards and wainscot for more than two hundred years. From late spring to late summer the sun is high enough in the sky to reach an area of the stencil next to the first floor dining room for about fifteen minutes each day, just as it did in 1785 when the house was built. Although, using visual clues and fragments in order to reconstruct in imagination the past has its limits, walls have a fixed surface area and fixed patterns can be mapped on the gaps and lost fragments. On one wall there is a fragment from an arch and from that small clue I can reconstruct the pattern of the whole wall. From the other fragments – a flake of paint or a broken shutter – I can reconstruct the appearance of the whole wall as it would have looked two hundred years ago.

∗

The subject of English 18th-century stencil wall decoration is a much unexplored area of design history. Apart from articles written in *The Archaeological Journal* in 1938 and 1940 by Frances Reader, there have been no other published articles which specifically deal with the subject. Although stencilling is occasionally mentioned in books on architectural history,[1] the only recent analysis of the subject is four pages in *The Shell Book of the Home in Britain* by James Ayres[2].

The most obvious reason for this lack of study is the scarcity of visible remains. Most stencils have been obliterated by successive layers of wallpaper, replastering and more generally by demolition and renovation of the buildings in which they were painted. This process of change and destruction has always been greater in cities. Thus London now has only five known examples, whereas Frances Reader provides three examples from the small market town of Saffron Walden in Essex[3]. By 1940 there were nine recorded patterns in England from Buckinghamshire, Gloucestershire, Essex and Kent. Although James Ayres provides useful information on stencilling technique, all the examples he provides are from the early 19th century. The Victoria and Albert Museum has no examples of 18th century stencils. Nevertheless, there are at least two in Saffron Walden museum.[4] Further research, based on an examination of local history collections together with photographic documentation of examples *in situ* would provide a much more detailed and comprehensive assessment of the ranges and techniques of 18th century stencilling. At the moment, in terms of research, we are still in 1940. Despite the scarcity of visible remains, the fact that there are examples from widely dispersed locations suggests that it was widespread in the late 18th century.

There are many recorded examples of stencils from the Middle Ages until the 17th century. Referring to Derbyshire, Addy writes,

"Before the introduction of wallpaper it was usual to decorate walls with leaves with rather
indistinct stems. This was done by means of a contrivance resembling a large stencil plate.
The practice is ancient whether the stencil plate was used anciently or not."[5]

As to the precise technique of stencilling and the composition of paint pigments, there are very few
references in medieval literature. Like many other trades, the guilds jealously guarded the secrets of
their trade. The Painter Stainers' Company had a monopoly on all decorative painting in the City of
London.[6] By the late 17th century, it was a very hierarchical profession, ranging from artistic
supervisors, such as Sir James Thornhill, to the people who washed brushes and prepared pigments.
Stencilling was discouraged by the Painter Stainers' Company, described as

"a false and deceitful work and destructive of the art of painting, being a great hinderer of
ingenuity and a cherisher of idleness and laziness in all aspects in the said art."[7]

This perhaps explains why there are no known examples of stencilling from the late 17th to the late
18th century. Ayres suggests that it is unlikely that the practice completely died out between 1700
and 1790 in either England or America.[8] From the 17th century onwards, wallpaper increasingly
became the preferred method of wall decoration. Decorative painting in the houses of the wealthy
became less elaborate after the decline of the Baroque style in the 1730s. As Pears writes;

"When grandiose decorative schemes became less fashionable and such teams of painters less
frequent, the effect was to increase the separation between the varieties of painter. Decorative
schemes continued, of course, but the tendency was for them to become more modest in size
and to be confined to specific areas surrounded by frames . . . the remainder of the work was
carried on by the house painters working of necessity on the site, with much less need or
opportunity for performing tasks which required artistic accomplishment."[9]

Thus, the increasing division of labour in the industry as a whole meant that a variety of tasks
which had previously been the exclusive prerogative of the painter, such as the preparation of
pigments, were now provided by specialist colour shops. As Robert Campbell put it in *The London
Tradesman* (1747);

"This branch [House painting] is now at a very low ebb, on account of the methods practised
by some colour shops, who have set up mills to grind the colours, sell them to noblemen and
gentlemen ready mixed at a low price."[10]

Pears mentions that colourmen first appeared in the 1690s and that by the 18th century, paint
was an exported commodity.[11] Campbell regarded painting as a lowly profession and warned parents
against sending their sons into this trade:

"The Journey men of this Branch are the dirtiest, laziest and most debauched Set of fellows
that are of any Trade in and about London. Therefore I think no Parent ought to be so mad
as to bind his Child Apprentice for Seven Years, to a Branch that may be learned almost in

as many Hours, in which he cannot earn a subsistence when he has got it, runs the Risk of breaking his Neck every Day, and in the end turns out a mere Blackguard."[12]

Thus, in the 18th century, house painting became an increasingly de-skilled and low-status occupation.

★

Despite protests, the Painter Stainers' Company was unable to maintain its control of the house painters' trade. The expansion of London beyond the city walls, the growth of speculative building, specialisation and de-skilling of labour; these factors meant that all the medieval guilds associated with the building trade became increasingly irrelevant to the physical growth of London in the 18th century. Pears writes;

> "The mystery of house painting had always lain as much in the preparation of the colours as it did in their application. The growth of a paint industry removed this skill, so that house painters no longer had a monopoly to retail but had only their labour power left."[13]

Nevertheless, even in 1786, the Painter Stainers' Company was upholding its rights in the City. Englefield mentions that in this year a foreigner was prosecuted for exercising the art of painting in the City, and he was "admonished not to exercise the business in future without being naturalised and made free".[14] While the Company was still upholding its rights in the City, there was little it could do about the growing areas beyond the city boundaries. Even so, it is quite possible that a member of the Company painted the stencils at 53 Cross Street. Campbell states that house painters were out of work for a large part of the year.

> "Their Work begins in April or May and continues until the Return of the Company to Town in Winter, when there are many of them out of Business."[15]

Even though stencilling was viewed with disfavour by the Masters of the Company, the possibility of finding work as a stenciller would have been desirable, particularly in winter, as interior work did not depend on the vagaries of the weather. As there are no published records of the organisation of the stencillers' trade in England, I can only suggest a number of possibilities. If the stenciller had been working according to the rules and regulations of the Painter Stainers' Company, it is possible to estimate the cost of painting the stencil. It was probably painted in 1785, the year the house was built. The evidence is that it was directly painted onto the finished and flatted plaster surface – there are no other layers of paint. The stone colour which forms the first layer of paint on the primed and clearcoled surface of the wainscot in the hall exactly matches the stone colour ground of the stencil, and given the wide variations in stone colour at the time (due to variations in pigments and preparation), it seems highly probable that they were painted at the same time.

Two years before the stencil was painted, the Painter Stainers' Company set new prices for house painting because

"... the prices which had been generally charged for the different kinds of house painting were the same as they had been for many years past" and "the prices of the materials used in the trade had of late years greatly advanced, and still remained at a very high price."[16]

The prices are organised according to piecework, which was the preferred method of payment by house painters.[17] The most expensive mentioned is

"on wall Painting four times in oil and once flatted white on stucco, per yard 15d."[18]

According to *The New Practical Builder* (1823), flatting refers to the white-lead-based first coat of paint:

"The Nottingham white lead is the most esteemed for what is called flatting, or dead-white ... This composition, if genuine, improves by keeping, and for the best whites it should be, at least, two or three years old".[19]

Where the Cross Street stencil is chipped, one can see that the flatted surface is still chalky white. The stencil contains five rather than four different colours, and as painting three times in oil was a penny less, five times was probably charged at a penny more – 16d per yard.

It was painted in distemper rather than oil. However, painting in both media was probably charged at the same rate by the Company since the painters in oil and the stainers in distemper received equal status when their guilds were merged in 1502.[20] This would not have been cheaper than an equivalent wallpaper. Although the most expensive wallpapers were as much as 8s a yard, Wells-Cole also mentions Chippendale's cathedral Gothic paper hung in the back staircase of Sir William Robinson's house in London at a price of 3¹/₂d a yard in the 1760s. The price of this wallpaper, of a similar design to the stencil, is a useful comparison to the prices charged by the Painter Stainers' Company for painting directly on the wall surface since it would be considerably cheaper than painting according to the rules of the Company. Indeed, Wells-Cole mentions that it was cheaper to plaster new walls for paper hangings than to prepare them to receive paint.[21] At this stage of my research, I do not know whether the preparing of the plaster surface was the responsibility of the plasterer or the stenciller, though if it was part of the same job it would have a direct bearing on the price.

Most accounts of stencilling have emphasised that it was cheaper than wallpaper.[22] Although much stencil work that survives is primitive, and was therefore cheaper to produce than even the cheapest wallpaper (especially since the wallpaper tax was not applicable), the design of the stencil at 53 Cross Street is comparatively sophisticated, forming a complete covering of the plaster in five different colours (some of the pigments such as the blue being quite expensive). The only other comparable 18th-century example that I have seen is from 15 Market Hill, Saffron Walden. Thus, the possibility that the stencil at Cross Street was chosen for stylistic reasons rather than simply because it was cheaper than wallpaper opens up some interesting questions on the reasons for the revival of stencilling in the late 18th century. I will return to this subject later. Nevertheless, it is highly unlikely that the stencil was painted according to the prices set by the Painter Stainers' Company. As Campbell puts it,

> "a house may be painted by any common labourer at one third the expense that it would have cost before the mystery was made public There are vast Numbers of Hands that follow this Branch, as it may be learned in a month as well as in Seven Years: Plasterers, Whitewashers, and everybody that can but handle a brush, now set up for House Painters."[23]

✶

If the study of 18th century wall stencils is virtually non-existent in Britain, this is not the case in America. Frances Reader's pioneering article on English mural decoration refers glowingly to the work of Janet Waring who recorded over eighty examples of 18th and 19th-century stencils in America, the earliest being from 1778. In her book *Early American Stencils on Walls and Furniture* (1937), Waring writes,

> "A majority of the settlers in the section where stencilled walls remain were of English ancestry and their memories and cultural traditions reached back to the shires of England, especially to East Anglia."[24]

Thus, research on American wall stencils is relevant to England, since practitioners from England would have taken their craft to America.

More recently, American studies of wall stencilling have become part of the wider project of 'Folk Studies' in which rural crafts and traditions are celebrated, recorded and revived. An example of this approach is *Early American Wall Stencils in Colour* (1976), in which stencilling is described as "an ancient tool developed in a special Yankee way".[25] It mentions that there are only fifteen known American stencillers from the 18th and 19th centuries (all but one with English surnames). The earliest printed reference to stencilling in America is an advertisement in a Baltimore newspaper in 1796 which reads,

> "Priest, William, Painter, interior Works. Painting in imitation of paper hangings, By a mechanical process, which from its facility, enables the artist to paint a room, staircase, &c, upon lower terms, than it is possible to hang with paper of equal beauty . . . He offers his services as above or in laying plain grounds in distemper with plain or festoon borders."[26]

This appears to confirm that stencilling was relatively cheaper than wallpaper although the equal beauty he refers to could be an advertising gimmick. The "mechanical process" is probably advertising hype. Oman and Hamilton[27] refer to the granting of patents in England for early wallpaper printing machines in the 1760s and 70s, so it is possible, though unlikely, that similar mechanical processes were also being developed in the practice of wall stencilling.

As yet there are no recorded examples of stencillers' advertisements in the provincial press in England, although it is probable that handbills were the most widely used form of advertisement for stencilling as is the case for other trades and services in the 18th century. No stencillers' handbills are known to have survived. In America, stencillers were often itinerant workers, travelling the turnpikes of the East coast along with peddlers, tinkers and salesmen. One early 19th-century stenciller, Moses Eaton, travelled across Maine and New Hampshire with "an adventurous artistic spirit".[28] His style is recognisable enough for the authors to locate specific examples of his work in houses across the area. Indeed, 78 of his stencil plates have been found together with his old stencil kit.

Another stenciller, Lydia Eldridge Williams, is the only known woman to have practised the craft. She stencilled her own home in Ashfleld, Massachusetts in the early 19th century. We can assume that some stencils in England would also have been created by enthusiastic home decorators, but at this stage we know neither their names nor gender. It is possible that stencilling was included amongst the accomplishments for middle-class women, such as sewing and piano playing, but it would not have been painted for money since women were barred from the Painter Stainers' Company as well as from all other guilds in the city of London. Nevertheless, the American evidence does suggest possible avenues of research for English stencils. Some study of stylistic variations and similarities in the existing stencil remains would allow for a more precise understanding of the itinerary of individual travelling stencillers, even if due to lack of written evidence, they are likely to remain anonymous.

✳

As to the precise technique of stencilling, the 18th century witnessed the growth of trade manuals such as Robert Dossie's *Handmaid to the Arts* (1764), and *The Complete Dictionary of Arts and Sciences* (1764, ed. T.H. Croker et al.). Such books made public what had formerly been the trade secrets of the medieval guilds. On the first page of the first volume, Dossie sets out his aim to teach,

"A perfect knowledge of the MATERIA PICTORIA, or, the nature, use, preparation and composition of all the various substances employed in PAINTING . . . "[29]

With reference to this text, and a few others from the 19th century, I will suggest the likely methods of preparation of the pigments used in the stencil at Cross St, the composition of the distemper and the technique of stencilling.

There are five colours in the stencil: white, stone colour, black, dark green and blue. As I have already mentioned, the pigments were probably bought ready prepared at a colour shop. The composition of stone colour is difficult to access, since even though it was a commonly used and cheap pigment in the 18th century, there are a variety of formulas mentioned in the primary sources of the period. Cruikshank and Burton[30] suggest that in the 18th and 19th century, stone colour generally referred to the warm yellowish hues of Bath stone rather than the grey tones of Portland stone, although there are inconsistencies in various texts. The pigment is not even mentioned in *Handmaid to the Arts*, although "yellow oker" is probably a different name for the same colour.

The New Practical Builder (1823) describes stone colour as a compound of "white with a little stone ochre".[31] Even though it does not describe the composition of stone ochre we can assume that it is similar to red ochre:

> "a native earth; but that which is in common use is coloured red by calculation, being yellow when dug out of the earth, the same with the yellow ochre commonly used. This latter substance is chiefly brought from Oxfordshire, where it is found in great abundance".[32]

Indeed Vanherman in *Every Man his own House Painter* (1829), suggests that stone colour may be prepared with road dust.[33] Thus, even in the early 19th century, not all paints were prepared by specialist colour shops. The stone colour has a slight greenish tinge which was probably created by the application of a small amount of verdigris in the pigment.

According to *The New Practical Builder* (1823), there are two main forms of black pigment:

> "Lamp-black is properly the soot of oil collected as it is formed by burning; but, generally, no other than a soot raised from the resinous and fat parts of fir-trees.

> "Ivory-black is composed of fragments of ivory or bone, burnt to a black coal, in a crucible or vessel, from which all access of air is excluded and then ground very fine for use."[34]

Since lamp-black is the only form of black mentioned in Smith's *The Art of Painting in Oyl* (1705), and that it was probably slightly cheaper to produce than ivory black, the Cross Street stencil probably contains lamp-black pigment.

Lamp-black was also probably used in the preparation of the pigment for the dark green colour in the stencil. Indeed, it is so dark that from a distance it is difficult to distinguish it from the black. Whether it was originally brighter in tone can only be ascertained by detailed paint analysis in a laboratory. Green, or verdigris as it is often styled in the 18th century, was one of the more expensive pigments. Cruikshank and Burton[35] refer to a Colourman's price list of 1744 in which common pigments such as stone and lead white are sold at 4d or 5d a lb whereas Prussian blue and green cost between 8d and 12d per lb. These prices are almost the same as the prices quoted by Taylor in *The Builders Price Book* of 1776 and 1787.[36]

According to all accounts of verdigris, it is "an oxide of copper, formed by a vegetable acid" (*The New Practical Builder*).[37] Some accounts also refer to the practice of mixing it with vinegar. Dossie writes,

> "Verdigris, though used with water colours, cannot, nevertheless, be brought to a paper state for working by means of water. The method of rendering it fit to be used in water colours is to powder it, and then to pour on it a quantity of vinegar . . . This vinegar, when it has dissolved as much of the verdigris as it can take up, must be poured off free from the settlings or undissolved part of the verdigris and must be put into a bottle to be kept for use."[38]

If the preparation of verdigris seems somewhat complicated, the appendix to volume two of

Handmaid to the Arts contains the fascinating but tortuous recipe of Doctor Woodward for the preparation of Prussian blue pigment;

> "Take any quantity of blood and evaporate it to dryness, continuing the heat until it become black . . ."[39]

A number of other processes and ingredients are added including "vitriol" and "pearl ashes" which turn the mixture to a green sediment.

> "Add spirit of salt to it afterwards . . . and the green matter will then soon appear to be converted into a beautiful blue."[40]

It is more than likely that whoever painted the stencil bought it as a prepared pigment rather than following these lengthy instructions.

The remaining colour used in the stencil is lead white. *The New Practical Builder* describes it as

> "the principal ingredient used in house painting; and this is a calx obtained by rolling sheets of lead into coils, with their surfaces, about half an inch distant from each other, and then placing them vertically in earthen pots, with a portion of good vinegar at the bottom, in such a way that, when set in a moderate heat, the vapour of the vinegar corrodes the lead, so that the external portion will come off in white flakes when the lead is beaten or uncoiled. These flakes being bleached, ground, and saturated with linseed oil, form the 'white lead' of the shops."[41]

Lead paint was always one of the most hazardous pigments to prepare and use and it was the main cause of blindness among workers in the paint industry. Indeed, Englefield mentions that the Painter Stainers' Company became sole administrators of a charity for blind pensioners in 1784.[42] Even so, many painters who became blind or sick, particularly if they were not members of the Company, would have fallen through the safety net of charity and ended up as beggars or simply starved. Dossie mentions that workers involved in paint production normally did not survive for longer than a dozen years.

In order to make distemper, the prepared pigments were mixed with size (made from boiled rabbit bones) and water. For stencil work the consistency had to be finely tuned – too thin would mean paint dribbling down the wall; too thick would mean unnecessary expense. As to the precise technique of wall stencilling there are no published 18th-century accounts. Indeed it is likely that after the technique fell into disfavour in the 17th century stencilling was exclusively used in the manufacture of wallpaper. Some of the earliest wallpapers were produced by means of stencil. It was always the cheapest method of production. Dossie mentions that the other two techniques were wood block printing and the application of "the pencil" (i.e. hand painting).

On stencilling in wallpaper design, Dossie writes

> "In the common kinds of wallpaper, it is usual to print only the outlines and to lay on the rest of the colours by stencilling, which both saves the expense of cutting prints and can be done by common workmen."[43]

He suggests that stencils should be cut from oiled paper. Pencilling, the third of the techniques he describes, is only used for detailed work:

"It is most frequently used for those parts of the design, where a spirit of freedom and variety not to be had in the printed outlines is desired to be in the work."[44]

As I have already mentioned, the white lead colour in the stencil at 53 Cross St has been painted by hand and it certainly does add "a spirit of freedom and variety".

The earliest published guide to the technique of wall stencilling is to be found in the Nathanial Whittock's *Decorative Painters and Glaziers' Guide* of 1827. In this book he describes stencilling as "the cheapest and expeditious method of decorating rooms". He goes on to describe the technique:

"The usual way of proceeding is to produce an elegant pattern, containing about four colours . . . The stenciller must be careful to trace upon transparent paper . . . all the outlines of the subject that is in middle tint; he will on another piece of tracing paper draw the outline of the first shade, and on a third the darkest shade and on the fourth the strongest lights. When the tracing of the whole is made, they must be transferred to common thin paste board . . . then cut with a penknife."[45]

✱

From what I can ascertain from a visual examination of the stencil at 53 Cross St, the ground colour is stone. Upon this are laid three separate stencils on top of each other in the order of Prussian blue, lamp-black and blackish verdigris. The final details are hand-painted in lead white.

Stylistically, the Cross Street stencil is closer to contemporary examples of wallpaper rather than other wall stencils. As I have already mentioned, in terms of technique, the only other 18th-century stencil I have seen that comes close to the one at Cross Street is an example discovered in 1916 at 15 Market Hill, Saffron Walden and described by Frances Reader in 1940.[46] Reader writes,

"It is a remarkably rich decoration, simply produced by two stencils, green and white on a dark blue ground. The designer of this pattern had evidently explored the possibilities of his craft with great success, and has skilfully made use of the outlines of the details, so as to avoid an excess of the 'ties' which form the great defect of much stencil work."[47]

As to the size of the stencil plates required, I have based my measurements on the basic units which are repeated vertically in the Market Hill example at an approximate measurement of 27cm x 27cm and in the Cross Street example at the same measurement in 'drop' repeats. Presumably the stencil plates would have been somewhat larger (approximately 1 foot square). A comparison with the units of measurement of the other stencils would be a useful exercise, since they could then be plotted as ratios to the wall surface on which they were applied. With reference to wallpaper, Wells-Cole writes,

"How far was the choice of a large or small pattern directed by convention or an accepted

standard of taste? This has never before been systematically investigated ."[48]
The height from the dado rail to the plaster cornice in the hall at Cross St varies between 168 cm on the ground floor, to 156 cm on the first floor, allowing for approximately six repeated patterns at any one vertical plane.

The largest motif within the stencil pattern at Cross Street is the columned arch. Since the height of the columns is 9cm and the radius of the arches is also 9cm, it conforms to the proportions of a Palladian arch, even if it does contain Gothic details. From contemporary perspective, it might seem strange that a design should include both Classical and Gothic elements. However, the Gothic style in the 18th century was often superimposed on Classical forms. The title of Batty Langley's *Gothic Architecture Improved by Rules and Proportions* (1742), is indicative of the 18th-century approach to the Gothic. In this book, Langley proposes a sixth, Gothic order to add to the five Classical orders. Later building design books such as Pain's *The Practical Builder* (1774), combine elements of Palladian, Gothic and the fashionable Adam style.

In architectural terms, 53 Cross Street is a typical example of a modest, speculatively built terraced house of the 1780s. Judging from its ground-floor area, the house was a Third rate property by the Grades introduced with the 'Great Building Act' of 1774. First rate houses cost £850 or more, Second rate £300 or more, Third rate between £150 and £300 and Fourth rate less than £150[49]. Even though the house was modest it was also fashionable. It contains elements of Neo-Classicism such as the Grecian Doric pediment and pilasters at the front door, and the emphasis is on simple linearity in the architraving throughout the interior. Indeed, the only arch that is in the house is in the hall and the most elaborate mouldings in wood are the dentils above the front door and on the fireplace in the back, ground-floor parlour. The Adam influence is most clearly evident in the arabesque plaster mouldings of the frieze in the front ground-floor room, and the honeysuckle frieze on the *piano nobile* (the first floor).

Thus the Gothic stencil in the hall is merely one element in a variety of late 18th-century stylistic influences which can still be seen throughout the house. When these styles are seen in the context of subsequent design influences, such as the austere Regency marble-effect wallpaper, the Art Nouveau fingerplate that I found under the floorboards, the 1950s bed-sit sink units that are still in many of the rooms and the 1980s punk murals, the house becomes a cacophony of different design elements. Nevertheless each aspect of the design of the house has been chosen for specific reasons and within the technological and cost constraints and the cultural possibilities of the time.

★

The late eighteenth century is often regarded as a crucial 'turning point' in history, whether as the beginning of the Industrial Revolution (Blanqui),[50] the consumer revolution,[51] the beginnings of mass production (Forty),[52] or more generally an 'epistemic break' between classical and modern forms of power (Foucault).[53] The very notion that there are crucial 'breaks' in history is now challenged by revisionist historians. In a decade when the Post War Settlement disintegrates politically, economically and geographically, the periodisation of even the 20th century has become a subject of contested meanings and interpretation.

Even such shibboleths as the Industrial Revolution are no longer taken for granted by historians. Recently, revisionists have questioned the 'industrial revolution' for very similar reasons that the term 'consumer revolution' is rejected.[54] It is argued that many of the social changes associated with industrialism – such as the division of labour and the expansion of the urban population – occurred well before its advent. Certainly, the shift from medieval guild practices towards 'free market' labour relations in the house painters' trade date from the late 17th/early 18th century. Equally, industrialism in the eighteenth century was confined to the cotton industry[55]; all the techniques used to paint the stencil at Cross Street were widely used in the middle ages. Thus there is little evidence of the material consequences of the first stage of the industrial revolution at Cross Street (except perhaps for a pair of cotton working-man's stockings that I found in a wall cavity).

Nevertheless I would argue that term 'industrial revolution' is useful, since it marks the beginnings of what Hobsbawm refers to as "self sustained economic growth"[56], which was to have enormous impact throughout society. even if it was only dimly appreciated at the time. This is not to suggest that all aspects of 18th-century society were embryonic forms of the present, merely that history cannot 'recreate' the past. The historian can only search for traces and fragments, some of which are open to contemporary forms of understanding (Positivist, Marxist, post-modern etc.). Arguing from a Marxist perspective, Hobsbawm writes in *The Age of Revolution*,

> "some time in the 1780s, and for the first time in human history, the shackles were taken off the productive powers of human societies, which henceforth became capable of the constant, rapid and up to the present limitless multiplication of men, goods and services . . . no previous society had been able to break through the ceiling which a pre-industrial social structure, defective science and technology, and consequently periodic breakdown, famine and death, impose on production."[57]

Although the term 'Industrial Revolution' was not used until the 1830s, Hobsbawm argues that it is an important concept because it describes the beginning of a process which has not been completed:

> "If the sudden, qualitative and fundamental transformation, which happened in or about the 1780s, was not a revolution then the word has no common sense meaning. The Industrial Revolution was not indeed an episode with a beginning and an end. To ask when it was 'complete' is senseless, for its essence was that henceforth revolutionary change became the norm."[58]

Since the house was built four years before the French Revolution, and I do not wish to embroil myself in the class debate of the 18th century, I prefer to use the term 'middling sort' rather than 'middle class' when referring to the original occupants of the house. The term only excludes the aristocracy/gentry (who would have lived in a bigger house), and the 'lower sort' (who probably painted the stencil). Nevertheless, at least one member of the household chose to have a stencil painted in the hall at 53 Cross Street (it was numbered 23 until 1864, according to the Islington trade directories). According to information kindly supplied by Rachael Short the Poor Rate records show that Thomas Vernon lived in the house from 1787 until 1791 and Richard Wyatt from 1795 until 1805. However there is no record of their occupations.

The term 'middling sort' is useful since its vagueness matches my knowledge of who the original occupants of 53 were. Indeed, apart from stylistic clues, the only evidence that I have for dating the building of the house to 1785 is a piece of unprimed deal moulding that I found in a wall cavity in the front ground-floor room wrapped in a pair of cotton working men's stockings. Written on the piece of wood was, "George Shaw went to Aameica [sic] March 1785". The fact that it was still covered in wood shavings suggests that George Shaw was involved in the building of the house and that it had remained untouched since the house was built.

★

Whatever their differences in interpretation, historians are in agreement that there was a wide variety of commodities available for the consumer of the 'middling sort' in the late 18th century. I will now address the question of why the particular design of the stencil was chosen and why it was a stencil rather than the more typical choice of wallpaper.

In the late 18th century; the repertoire of mural decoration in most terraced houses was set by the wallpaper industry. Throughout this century Britain was a world leader in the production of wallpaper, challenged only by France in the second half of the century. Oman and Hamilton give figures for the export of British wallpapers in 1774 which show that

"the industry was in a very flourishing condition and . . . British stained papers were appreciated all over the known world."[59]

An indication of the range of wallpapers on offer is provided by a trade card of the 1760s.[60] It offers wallpapers in "the Modern, Gothic or Chinese tastes". Gothic wallpaper was nearly always hung in halls. One of the earliest examples was in Horace Walpole's house at Strawberry Hill and dates from 1749.

In 1749, Walpole described his Gothic hall in a letter to a friend:

"under two arches you come to the hall and staircase, which it is impossible to describe to you, as it is the most particular and chief beauty of the castle . . . my house is so monastic . . . I have a little hall decked with long saints, on lean arched windows . . . Imagine the wall covered with (I call it paper, but it is really paper painted in perspective, to represent) Gothick fretwork."[61]

When I visited Strawberry Hill I got a sense of how the hall looked in 1749. Unfortunately the original paper, a fragment of which is framed at the foot of the staircase, is now replaced by a salmon pink and white approximation of the original which gives little sense of the "Gothick gloomth" that Walpole intended. Interestingly Oman and Hamilton mention that at one point Walpole considered having it coloured but eventually decided that it was superfluous, preferring the grisaille effect of the stone colour.[62]

By the 1760s, Gothic paper was widely available and advertised. The Ancient High House in Stafford has an example from circa 1760. Like the stencil at Cross Street, it contains both Classical and Gothic elements. Lynn mentions that in America in the 1760s the Gothic style was frequently mentioned in advertisements for wallpapers.[63] These were mostly imported from England and nearly always recommended for use in halls.

Lynn also writes about 'pillar and arch' papers:

"One distinctly English wallpaper style probably originated during the 1760s continued in vogue in America throughout the turn of the 19th century . . . called 'pillar and arch patterns' by the 18th century trade, these patterns featured a round-headed arch carried on two columns or pillars. These architectural elements framed a central motif, usually a single figure, a group of figures, an urn, or a vase holding flowers. One or two motifs were repeated one over another, and side by side or were drop repeated."[64]

Thus, the design source of the stencil at Cross Street combines elements of both Gothic and the more purely Classical pillar and arch wallpaper patterns. Although the stencil has a three-dimensional quality, it is closer in its 'flat' perspective to stucco relief wallpaper (of the type hung in Strawberry Hill), rather than the deeper perspectives of the pillar and arch examples.

There might be a more ancient design provenance for 'pillar and arch' patterns. In *A Classification of Tudor Domestic Wall-Paintings*,[65] Reader provides examples of different types of wall painting from the 16th century. One type referred to is the 'arcaded façade'. She writes,

"Paintings in this class are mainly of [an] . . . essentially architectural character. Those in important houses are a representation of a fully developed classic façade with columns, arches, frieze and panelled plinth richly ornamented, with figures, seascapes, etc., in rich colouring."[66]

It is quite possible that the 'pillar and arch' wallpapers of the second half of the 18th century were in fact a revival of an older form of mural decoration, and that the use of this design in the stencil at Cross Street is an example of the revival of its direct application onto the wall surface, albeit on a different scale and with the use of stencils rather than the brush alone. An example from Siwards End, Saffron Walden mentioned by Reader shows that both stencilling and the 'pillar and arch' design were to be found in at least one 16th-century wall painting, even though the scale is much larger than the Cross St stencil (about 9ft between each column), Although the colours are not reproduced, there was a tradition dating from before the 16th century that wall painters ('plasterers')

"were restricted to the use of six colours only, 'mingled with size only, and not with oil', and they were forbidden the use of varnish, 'either mixed with the paint or as a glazing'."[67]

It was not until the 19th century that oil paint and varnish were widely used in wall stencils. The Cross St stencil, with its five distemper colours, certainly conforms to medieval traditions, even if the conditions in which it was produced had changed dramatically.

By the 18th century, 'pillar and arch' and Gothic wallpaper designs tended to be recommended for use in halls and staircases. There are a few examples of Gothic wallpaper in dining rooms and parlours, but by the second half of the 18th century this was the exception rather than the rule. Throughout the 17th and 18th centuries the domestic interior became more specialised and the design of its subdivided spaces (halls, parlours etc.) more specific.

Foreign visitors to England in the 18th and early 19th century were frequently amazed by the attention paid to the decoration of the hall. Cruikshank quotes a Frenchman, Louis Simond, who commented,

> "instead of the abominable filth of the common entrance and the common stairs of a French house, here you step from the very street on a neat floor cloth, the walls papered or painted, a lamp in its glass bell hanging from the ceiling."[68]

Summerson quotes another part of Simond's *Journal of a Tour of residence in Great Britain* (1817), in which he expresses his fascination with the English practice of living vertically, rather than the usual horizontal manner of the French;

> "These narrow houses, three or four storeys high – one for eating, one for sleeping, a third for company, a fourth under ground for the kitchens, a fifth perhaps at top for the servants – and the agility, the ease, the quickness with which the individuals of the family run up and down, and perch on the different storeys, give the idea of a cage with its sticks and birds."[69]

At 53 Cross Street, the ground-floor back parlour may now be a bedroom, the kitchen now a bathroom, and the grandest room in the house a sub-divided kitchen and dining room, but the hall serves exactly the same function as it did when the house was built – getting its inhabitants from one 'perch' to another.

★

I have already briefly alluded to the generally accepted view that in the 18th century wall stencilling was considered a cheap alternative to wallpaper. The wallpaper tax is also cited as the chief incentive behind the choice of stencilling. Yet wallpaper tax was imposed in 1712 and wall stencils did not reappear until the late 18th century. Clearly, for most of the 18th century the tax did not discourage people from buying wallpaper, even though there was widespread avoidance of paying the tax both by the manufacturer and through other means, by the consumer. For instance Oman and Hamilton mention:

> "By decorating rooms with white paper and afterwards having it painted it was possible to elude the vigilance of the excise officers, who stamped all wallpapers produced at the authorised

factories. As late as 1778, special instructions had to be issued to the excise officers to search for this sort of fraud against the revenue."[70]

Sometimes plain wallpaper was stencilled and this gives an indication of the immediate origins of the revival of stencilling directly onto the wall surface.

The wallpaper tax was introduced in 1712 at 1d per yard and raised by $^1/_4$d in 1714, in order to help finance the costs of war. In 1777 it was raised further to the price of 1 $^3/_4$d (in addition to a licence fee of £20 per annum to wallpaper producers),[71] as part of the range of harsh economic measures imposed by the government to pay for the war with the American colonies. The fact that the war had been lost fuelled widespread resentment towards the government throughout society. It was the first major defeat for Britain in over a century. As Langford puts it;

> "The economic problems to a nascent industrial society by a world war and the accompanying embargoes on trade were immense . . . Unprecedentedly high taxes and the rapid growth of the national debt reinforced the financial crisis and created serious economic problems. Fundamental questions were raised about government, parliament, and the political system generally."[72]

The widespread antipathy towards the established order was also expressed in the Gordon Riots of 1780 and in other less violent ways. Tax avoidance was an issue much discussed in the House of Commons throughout the 1780s as well as the problem of smuggling, that most famous form of import tax avoidance in the 18th century.

In his contribution to *The Birth of a Consumer Society*, John Brewer analyses the connection between the political radicalism in 18th-century England and its commercialisation, by potters, publicans and printers. He writes,

> "The creation of a radical 'political culture' complete with its own forms of dress, types of food, and modes of celebration was not merely the creation of alternative means of political expression, but the expansion and diversification of a market for politics as a cultural commodity or product."[73]

It is possible that revival of the wall stencil in the late 18th century was another expression of political dissent as a 'cultural commodity', an 18th-century version of the contemporary politically informed consumerism represented by 'green consumerism', boycott of products from repressive regimes and the 'trade not aid' movement. Similarly, avoiding paying wallpaper tax may well have been informed by more than reasons of utility. Oman and Hamilton mention that in 1778, a petition was addressed to the Prime Minister begging him to extend the wallpaper tax to wall-painting, in order to 'crush' its revival.[74]

When looking at the reasons for the revival of stencilling in the late 18th century it is also important to look at questions of taste. If there is a necessary opacity in our understanding of 18th-century primary sources, there is a fog – or rather, a 19th-century industrial smog – that separates the contemporary historian from the question of late eighteenth-century taste. There is a certain received wisdom that the 18th-century Gothic revival prefigured Romanticism. Horace Walpole papered his hall with Gothic wallpaper, then dreamt about the hall and was inspired to write the first Gothic horror novel *The Castle of Otranto* (1765). His fascination with the strange and the bizarre are often seen as a consequence of his homosexuality, and his eccentricity. Yet such an assumption suggests that the taste for the Gothic in the 18th century was radically different from the dominant Classical taste of the period. As Marilyn Butler writes in *Romantics, Rebels and Reactionaries,*

> "This theory of a stable eighteenth-century Classicism evolved in the late nineteenth century: it is in fact the natural corollary of the concept of Romanticism, which was supposed to have superseded Classicism. It probably reflects a prejudiced, outdated and inaccurate stereotype of the late eighteenth century as an era of stasis rather than of rapid expansion and change."[75]

She suggests that both the Gothic and Classical tastes were different forms of the same cultural historicism in the 18th century. The Neo-classical, with its celebration of ancient Greek architecture and its Arcadian countryside, was connected to the Gothicist regard for the art and culture of the Middle Ages. Both forms stress simplicity and the rustic and were interchangeable as stylistic motifs. It was in this cultural context that the stencil design at Cross Street was chosen, even if the choice of wall stencilling rather than wallpaper may have had specifically political motivations.

★

The physical geography of Islington in the late 18th century gives a rural context for the tastes of its inhabitants and visitors. Islington was a rustic retreat from London.[76] Situated on the nearest high land to the City, it was a popular destination for day trips. Illustrated on page 69 is the first London painting by the German artist, George Scharf. Painted in 1816 it shows the environment in which 53 Cross Street was built. The house is shown directly beneath the Wren-style church spire of St Mary's and is surrounded by a pastoral scene. To the left, on the horizon is Wren's Baroque dome of Saint Paul's. Every single element of the painting suggests Arcadia, from the Classical forms of buildings to the Grecian style of the women's dresses. It presents a myth, or at least a Romantic idea, of Islington.

However, even in the late 18th century, Canonbury fields were bordered by the continuous 'ribbon development' of Upper Street and Lower Street (now Essex Road). Even the cows were part of the insatiable demands of the nearby city – they were brought to these fields by drovers from all over the country and would eat their last pasture at Canonbury before being taken down Upper Street and St John Street to be slaughtered at Smithfield Market. The fields around London provided an alternative vision of England to that of the city. In the late 18th and early 19th century, William Blake regularly walked across the fields to the North of London and for him it was here, rather in the "Babylonian" City that the "New Jerusalem" was to be built;

> "The fields from Islington to Marybone,
>
> To Primrose Hill and Saint John's Wood

Were builded over with pillars of gold,
And there Jerusalem's pillars stood.

Her little ones ran on the fields,
The Lamb of God among them seen,
And fair Jerusalem his bride,
Among the little meadows green."[77]

The Cross Street stencil remained exposed until the 1810s when it was covered by marble brick effect wallpaper. Following the Napoleonic wars, Islington was inexorably becoming part of the great urban sprawl of London. A terrace of houses and shops was built opposite number 53 from the 1820s, forever obscuring the fields in front of the house. William Hone's poem 'Islington 1827' describes the growing urbanisation;

"Thy fields, fair Islington! begin to bear
Unwelcome buildings, and unseemly piles;
The streets are spreading, and Lord knows where
Improvement's hand will spare the neighbouring stiles."[78]

An engraving from 1835 (see page 70), shows Islington as it looked before the fields in front of Cross Street started to be covered by the Canonbury estate. Even when it was engraved, the image was already nostalgic – it was probably based on an earlier drawing since it does not show the houses in front of number 53. Yet it clearly shows that 53 was by now at the edge of the urban conurbation of London. By the mid 19th century the physical geography of Islington was essentially as it is now – one of the most built-up boroughs in the country. By an extraordinary twist of fate, the stencil has survived underneath succeeding layers of wallpapers for over two hundred years. This has been an amazing piece of luck for posterity.

Water-colour by George Scharf (1788–1860), his first painting made in London. In the background, St Mary's Parish Church spire is immediately behind the Cross Street terrace later numbered 53–59. To their right are house in Upper Street. The large white house on the far left is Fisher House (demolished 1945) in Essex Road at the foot of Cross Street, with St Paul's Cathedral to its right in the distance.

The little bridge the girls are being assisted across at the southern end of the loop is on the site of Canonbury Road.

Bird's-Eye View of Islington from Canonbury Tower, engraving of 1835

A view of Islington similar to the Scharf painting, from a slightly different angle. Still rural, though now considerably more built-up, showing the last loop of the New River, with Willow Bridge in the centre and the bridge shown in the 1816 Scharf painting, to the left beside the trees. Essex Road is now built up but still passing through fields; Fisher House is probably the building shown above the distant cows with St Paul's in the distance.

Notes

1 Cruikshank and Burton 1990
2 Ayres 1981 pp 175-179
3 Reader 1938
4 Ayres 1981
5 quoted in Ayres p175
6 Pears 1988
7 quoted in Reader 1938
8 Ayres 1981
9 Pears 1988
10 Campbell 1747 p103
11 Pears 1988
12 Campbell 1747
13 Pears 1988
14 Englefield 1923
15 Campbell 1747 p104
16 Englefield 1923 p180
17 Ayres 1981 p178
18 Englefield 1923
19 Kelly 1823
20 Reader 1941
21 Wells-Cole 1983 p3
22 Reader 1938 p121, Cruikshank and Burton 1990 p165, Ayres 1981 p176
23 Campbell 1747

24 Waring 1937, quoted in Reader 1940 p93

25 Fjestul et al. 1976

26 quoted in Fjestul et al. 1976

27 Oman and Hamilton 1982 p.28

28 Fjestul et al. 1976

29 Dossie 1764

30 Cruikshank and Burton 1990 p185

31 Kelly 1823

32 Kelly 1823

33 mentioned in Cruikshank and Burton 1990

34 Kelly 1823 p416

35 Cruikshank and Burton 1990 p183

36 Taylor, I and J 1776

37 Kelly 1823 p415

38 Dossie 1764 vol 1 p183

39 Dossie 1764 vol 2 appendix

40 Dossie 1764 vol 2 appendix

41 Kelly 1823

42 Englefield 1923

43 Dossie 1764

44 Dossie 1764

45 Whittock 1827 quoted in Cruikshank and Burton p167

46 Reader 1940 p89

47 Reader 1940

48 Wells-Cole 1983 p5

49 Byrne 1986 p36

50 mentioned in Hobsbawm 1977

51 McKendrick et al. 1992

52 Forty 1986

53 Foucault 1977

54 Styles 1993

55 Hobsbawm 1977

56 Hobsbawm 1977

57 Hobsbawm 1977 p43

58 Hobsbawm 1977 p44

59 Oman and Hamilton 1982 p35

60 mentioned in Heal 1925

61 quoted in Mordant Crook 1973

62 Oman and Hamilton 1982 p28

63 Lynn 1980

64 Lynn 1980

65 Reader 1941

66 Reader 1941 p188

67 Reader 1941 p 185

68 quoted in Cruikshank and Burton 1990 p66

69 quoted in Summerson 1988 p45

70 Oman and Hamilton 1982

71 Reader 1938 p121

72 Langford and Morgan 1996 p158

73 McKendrick et al. 1992

74 Oman and Hamilton 1982 p28

75 Butler 1981

76 Richardson 1988 p9

77 quoted in Nesfield-Cookson 1990

78 William Hone's *Table Book* 1827 quoted in Muir 1988

Bibliography

Ayres, James *The Shell Book of the Home in Britain*, Faber and Faber, London 1981

Brewer, J. in McKendrick, N., Brewer, J., Plumb, J.H. *The Birth of a Consumer Society*, Europa, London 1992

Brewer, John and Porter, Roy (eds) *Consumption and the World of Goods*, Routledge, London 1993

Butler, Marilyn *Romantics, Rebels and Reactionaries*, London 1981

Byrne, Andrew *London's Georgian Houses*, The Georgian Press London 1986

Campbell, Robert *The London Tradesman*, London 1747

Croker, T.H. et al. *The Complete Dictionary of Arts and Sciences*, London 1764

Cruikshank, Dan and Burton, Neil *Life in the Georgian City*, Viking, London 1990

Dossie, Robert *Handmaid to the Arts*, London 1764

Englefield, W. *The History of the Painter-Stainers' Company of London*, Chapman and Dodd, London 1923

Entwisle, E.A. *The Book of Wallpaper*, Kingsmead Reprints, Bath 1970

Fjestul, A., Brown Schad, P., Marhoefer, B. *Early American Wall Stencils in Colour*, E.P. Dutton, New York 1976

Forty, Adrian *Objects of Desire*, Thames and Hudson, London 1986

Foucault, Michel *Discipline and Punish, The Birth of the Prison*, Thames and Hudson, New York 1977

Heal, Ambrose *London Tradesman's Cards*, London 1925

Hobsbawm, Eric *The Age of Revolution*, Abacus, London 1977

Hone, W. *Table Book of London*, London 1827

Kelly, Thomas *The New Practical Builder and Workman's Companion*, London 1823

Langford, Paul 'The Eighteenth Century' in ed. Morgan, Kenneth *The Oxford Illustrated History of Britain*, Oxford University Press 1996

Langley, Batty *Gothic Architecture Improved by Rules and Proportions*, London, 1742

Lynn, Catherine *Wallpaper in America*, The Barra Foundation, New York 1980

Mordant Crook, J. 'Strawberry Hill Revisited' (reprints of three articles in *Country Life 1973*)

Muir, Augustus *Andersons of Islington*, James and James, London 1988

Nesfield-Cookson, Bernard 'William Blake's Spiritual Four-Fold City' in Matthews, J. and Potter, C. (eds) *The Aquarian Guide to Legendary London*, The Aquarian Press, London 1990

Oman, Charles and Hamilton, Jean *Wallpapers, a History and Illustrated Catalogue of the Collection of the Victoria and Albert Museum*, Sotheby Publications, London 1982

Pain, William *The Practical Builder*, London 1774

Pears, Iain *The Discovery of Painting*, Yale, London 1988

Reader, Frances 'The Use of the Stencil in Mural Decoration' in *The Archaeological Journal* 1938

Reader, Frances 'Further Notes on the Use of the Stencil in Mural Decoration' in *The Archaeological Journal* 1940

Reader, Frances 'A Classification of Tudor Domestic Wall Painting' in *The Archaeological Journal* 1941

Richardson, John *Islington Past*, Historical Publications, Herts 1988

Simond, Louis *Journal of a Tour 1810–1811* (ed.Hibbert, Christopher) London 1968

Smith, John *The Art of Painting in Oyl*, London 1676

Styles, John 'Manufacturing, Consumption and Design in Eighteenth Century England' in eds Brewer, J. and Porter, R. *Consumption and the World of Goods*, Routledge, London 1993

Summerson, John *The Classical Language of Architecture*, Thames and Hudson, London 1963

Summerson, John *Georgian London*, Pimlico, London 1988

Taylor, I. and J. *The Builders Price Book*, London 1776, 1787

Vanherman, T. H. *Every Man His Own House Painter*, London 1829

Ware, Isaac *A Complete Body of Architecture*, London 1768

Waring, Janet *Early American Stencils on Walls and Furniture*, 1937

Wells-Cole, Anthony *Historic Paper Hangings*, Leeds City Art Galleries 1983

Whittock, Nathanial *Decorative Painters' and Glaziers' Guide*, London 1827